D0846735

my mother's last dance

To Fauzia

my mother's last dance
honor ford-smith

*Many many thanks
for your fine hospitality
love*

Sister Vision
Black Women and Women of Colour Press

ISBN 1-896705-12-X

1997 © Honor Ford Smith

Copyright. All rights reserved. No part of this book can be reproduced or transmitted in any form or by any means without permission in writing from the publisher, except in the case of reviews.

97 98 99 00 01 ML 6 5 4 3 2 1

Canadian Cataloguing in Publication Data

Ford-Smith, Honor
ISBN 1-896705-12-X

I. Title

PS8561.066M9 1996   C818'.54   C96-932081-7
                PR9199.3.F5694M9 1996

Sister Vision Press acknowledges the financial support of the Canada Council and the Ontario Arts Council towards its publishing program.

Cover painting; cover & book design: *Stephanie Martin*
Author photo*: Maria LaYacona*
Printed & bound in Canada by *Metrolitho*

Represented in Canada by *The Literary Press Group*
Distributed by *General Distribution Services*
Distributed in the USA by *LPC Group/INBOOK*
Distributed in Britain by *Turnaround Limited*

Published by:
Sister Vision: Black Women and Women of Colour Press
P.O. Box 217, Station E
Toronto, Ontario, Canada M6H 4E2
Tel: (416) 595-5033
e-mail: sisvis@web.net

In memory of my mother
Joyce Kathleen Tate
1919 – 1994

Foreword

MY SINCERE THANKS to the institutions that supported this work. Among them are:

Amherst College for the Copeland Fellowship; The Bunting Institute at Radcliffe College; The Canada Council, The Toronto Arts Council, The Women and Development Unit of the University of the West Indies.

I am indebted to my editor Rhonda Cobham-Sander, for her patience, humour and wise counsel.

I also want to thank several people whose help was invaluable:

Jaqui Alexander, Peggy Antrobus, Deb Barndt, Pauline Cameron, Ted Chamberlain, Charmaine Dayle, Kari Dehli, Bernardo Garcia Dominguez, Elfreda Gordon, May Grant, Amy Gottlieb, Ketu Katrak, Pamela MacPherson, Stephanie Martin, Mervyn Morris, Sherene Razack, Kathleen Rockhill, Julie Salverson, Dennis Scott, Makeda Silvera, Roger Simon, Marguerite Tate and Osmond Tomlinson.

~

What follows is a mixture of fable, memory, fantasy and fact and is not a literal or factual representation of my family's history or anyone else's.

Contents

MY MOTHER'S LAST DANCE

History's Posse

Family
Portraits

Anna Taurus

"She's crazy"
they always said.

It's true that
in Hope Gardens one night
she unlocked and opened
the cages of the lioness and the wild bull.

Then they said
"She is the child of witchcraft
and obeah conceived in mid-atlantic
on a ship."

Isolated
she convulsed with her visions
her hurricane blew higher,
wider, quicker circles
seas rose up,
edges of mountains broke away.

The scientists said
"Avalanche in hot islands is unheard of,"
and wondered what caused the fall of snow
and earth on silenced tigers, iguanas and
the skeleton of a girl.

Cartography Of A Life
Grampa Son at Rockhall
In memory of Herbert 'Son' Tate (aka Manager) 1887–1947

Grampa didn't believe much in the past.
Said it didn't matter if your grandparents
were slaveowner and slave (as his were).
Said "Forget all that. History is history.
What you make of your life is up to you."
Hated being bossed so he left his job
as bookkeeper on somebody's estate
and leased hillside land in the St. Mary bush.
As day was lighting, the morning they arrived,
my uncle saw a family of clean ghosts dressed
to puss backfoot dining at a fiesta of the dead.
Tubercular and lockjawed, they smiled at Grampa Son,
and the processional of mule carts full of kin
welcoming them to Rockhall — graveyard of vanity.

Grampa's land sloped down to a level spot
where a man had built an ugly little house
barricaded by hills, with no view of road or gate.
My mother's room overlooked a graveyard.
No neighbours. Never a dry day. And the house
smelled of junjo all the time. No kerosene lamps
or kitchen bitches ever penetrated the close damp wool
of moonless nights alive with whistling frogs,

croaking lizards, mosquitoes, bullfrogs and
viral infections waiting to ambush the lung.

Plenty time breeze blew down the bananas,
but when the Abeng blew before day,
men, women and children still rolled out
to dig, plant, cut and carry banana.
Grampa was boss then and to him the rites of rank
seemed natural as the Rio Nuevo's flow,
only requiring stylish manoeuvre
just as driving the Devil's Racecourse
in the pouring rain required a science man
and a sideman shrewd as Anansi to get over,
to deliver the crop unharmed to New Works
before the whistle blew.

He rode a red mule called Phyllis.
Early o'clock, every morning she opened hostilities
as he went out to meet her. She kicked out
her hind legs and snorted, digging deep holes
in the wet earth of the yard. He grasped
the curb bit, jerked it back against her mouth
talking all the time. When she paused
for a second, he mounted her quickly.
Once in the saddle he controlled her absolutely.
He thought her wild, beautiful and well-gaited.
He loved her as he loved his accomplished amnesia
and thought he'd overcome without contamination
this history's poison in his blood.

Aunt May at Carron Hall Orphanage

For May Grant

Behind the school wall, routine replaced love.
As she learned her books, her few memories starved,
grew ragged where she kept them hidden:
the fragrance of mango the morning
her mother coughed herself to death;
waiting with her sister by the river
for a fish to bite her pin and thread ;
the beforeday buggy ride to the home,
her stiff fair-skinned Aunt, afraid to say
"this child is my sister's"
to the white missionaries
lest they find her black too
and turn her from benefactress
to object of their sanctifying mission.

Monday through Friday varied little
5:30 am: bell. Up to icy showers and dress.
6:30: bed making. 6:45: sweeping,
dormitory inspection. 7:30: line up.
Prayers. *O God please don't let me*
be a domestic. Please God, anything but that.
The missionaries marched through
the banana walk in academic gowns
The girls filed past the Reverend
answered "Present and good morning".

Uniform inspection (She was
in constant trouble with her hair
which never would submit.) Meals.
Classes in the science of cooking,
cleaning, laundering and home economy.

Then the Reverend and his daughter chose her
for adoption and experiment, moved her up to the manse.
Please God don't let me do anything wrong
Don't let these put me out too.
A set of physical practices re-made
and marked her body, created her desires.
Her sex itself, invisible, confined
or starved till metamorphosis.
Later, in the Scottish teacher's college,
something grew tough in her bone,
something sweet/sour and brittle as tamarind,
bitter as cerasee, sharp as Ping Wing Macca.
Accustomed to grow thirsty and in scorching sun,
it could bloom suddenly secretly at night,
a black flower white with rage.

Montreal Madonna and Child

On the floor of a Montreal apartment
A dark mother sits, holding her baby on her lap.
Behind her, Christmas tree lights blink
and a drooping white table cloth frames the pair.
The mother's breasts are round and large with milk,
her body curved and full. The child's tiny hands
are curled tight like boxer's gloves. Her large head
lolls in the woman's stiff arms. One-week-old eyes
stare straight ahead. The woman's neck is taut,
her mouth in shadow. There is no smile.
In the face of the child she loves is the presence
of the man she fears, the man who beat her
till she haemorrhaged. In the face of the innocent
is the anatomy of love's corpse — her torturer.

Lala the Dressmaker

In memory of Lascelles Tate, 1897 – 1967

Across from Chang's Green Emporium,
at Halfway Tree, near the fish fry sidewalk
where the men now sit to play at winning
crown and anchor — the dress shop circled her.
Inch measure of her life's scramble —
mountain range of checkered scraps
scent of fabric satin and taffeta —
on the wheels of the foot machines
tread-treading on the raw edges of
parties, teas and mothers' unions socials,
she was drawn into town, moving yard
by yard on the trains of bridal gowns,
fashioning a living from these things.
There was nothing else to do.

The rack of finished dresses, hanging, linings out,
concealed the beadwork her fingers were known for.
(A bald pink mannequin stood in the window —
Issa's had made it necessary.)
She, seated behind the children's magic mahogany
and glass case, cargo of the trade's beads, buttons,
zippers, a bangle, pencil, candle — even fruit,
finished collars. The firm fat of her hands
dissolved by time into a skein of thin brown linen.

One son. No husband. In silence
she stitched the distant canefield's cotton trees,
her shame-mi-lady face half-hidden by the shoulder length
crisp straightened hair. Occasionally, laughter
like a sluice-gate crinkled the black black eyes.

~

Once, before, in the town's taboo, Mohammed's
secret raft of tissue paper and bamboo stood among the
indentured ready to float back to him,
the Indian women chanting
"Allah man say husseh"
She earned her name Lala mingling with the chant
then breaking, climbing, tearing at the women's work
to see the forbidden centre of the thing.

And afterwards, the dry red heat of malaria,
journeying, fighting, fighting through the hot cloth
covering a sea of seaweed, to the place where
years later, behind the hidden patterns in the stripped
backroom of the shop, between rough walls
across the naked cedar table, she gambled on futures
staring into the muddled Darjeeling leaves
calling the good fortunes of the women to life.

~

History's Posse:
     Family Portraits

When Lala died
in the backroom of the shop
the girlchildren she had clothed,
whose futures she chose from those cupped in her hand
unpicked the beaded dresses to find what she hid
stitched in the lining.
They put the beads in the locks of their hair
their needles flashing (dangerous and quick)
collecting the light
opening
opening
their laughter strikes the centre of the clock
at Halfway Tree and the flames of the alleys
lick the rotten wooden walls.

Our Lady of Sorrows
Hope Road Triptych

I

After that Aunt Belle put all her bright colours to rest.
When her one-son Erdley died before his time,
she wore only those three mourning dresses — one grey
one navy blue and white, and one plain white cotton lace.
Day in, day out she would wear them,
rock herself on the veranda, look out at the cars
passing on Hope Road, cuss God's wickedness and cry.
And when the dresses were all washed out and torn up
and her heart was in such little pieces
that she could not breathe, so heavy
was the weight of her son's dead body on her chest,
she saw that though he would not rise
and come, his dead body could press heavier and heavier,
till the pieces of her heart became tiny specks of dust.
She died happily, and we buried her
in all her bright and boasty colours.

II

The dead daughter was the one Grandma loved the most,
the one whose picture she kept above the candy bottle
with the hot ginger sweets that burned you, the daughter
that died like a spite at twelve years old and was buried
in the grave with the alabaster angel to guard her. And then
Grandad went quick quick, so she said
and the bad feeling took her. So, if it is Saturday
we go with her to wash those graves so white
so white the ghosts have clean white homes
in the cemetery at Halfway Tree. And now Grandma
is wearing nightie and bed jacket all the time
and sitting on the veranda every evening, chanting
"I will go without a murmur ... " waiting for God
and the angels to come for her, the battered backless
King James in her hand. But every morning, she still
puts her hands on the big old radio at the 5 a.m. sign-on
when the evangelist from Minneapolis, Minnesota preaches —
in case there's really healing courtesy Radio Jamaica and Rediffusion.

Billy Boy, her black hair coiled like two snakes
on her forehead, won the upstairs house
opposite the governor's mansion in the Gore's terrazzo
tile factory raffle. The house always smelled of flowers
for Billy made her living from weddings, funerals, birthdays
and sicknesses. But after her husband shot himself
(by accident they said; cleaning his rifle, they said)
and her nieces burned to death in the fire at Gaiety Cinema
and her bad-boy grandson Arturo was shot to death
at sixteen for running a police roadblock,
she could never clean the smell of death out of the house.
One day Alsie her helper found that bending over the bath,
grating the coconut or cutting the flowers in the orchid house,
she could ketch myal and when her eyes turned inside out
all the familiar dead would take her hand, spin her
into the drums and blue and whisper warnings
and messages for all survivors on Hope Road.

A Message from Ni

They write so much about me now
that sometimes I read about myself
(hoping for strength, while I wait
among the the piles of empty shoes,
the still kisko carts and the mad warriors
in the sidewalk market at Halfway Tree)
I never recognize that woman they describe.
Let me tell you how it really was:

my body shook in battle.
and I vomited after seeing the dead
At first the smell of blood
made me faint. Blinded by a future
I could not vision, my old words meaningless,
choked to silence in a forest of trees
I had no names for, I fell and fell,
was lost, bled, marooned in a landscape
that grew stranger with each discovery I made.

Once for hours I climbed that cracked
crumbling black rock, till hunched up and
hungry I could stare down at the oceans of cane
bound by the sunlit grid of straight roads
and study the repetitious movements of slaves
Tied as I am to that treadmill of change,
I envied them obedience's freedom
I hungered for their assured meals

their chance to confuse imitation
with innovation, to trace all evil
to one source outside themselves.

At times like that I cursed the people
they say I led: when the Abeng blew
I longed for lovers or children or
invented dreams to fill the hollow
sleepless nights
        (the pumpkin seeds that overnight bore
        fruit to feed us was one, the bullets
        that I caught between mi legs and threw
        back at the enemy was another)

I told the others these dreams.
They repeated them. In their believing
I believed myself. That was all I had
to hold against surrender, to hold against
the defeat that would make me visible in
their history and I wanted that,
I was that vain.
How I prayed to be freed from what drove
me on: they never mention that, or
how close courage is to fear.
It was terror of terror that drove me on
till it was all over and I heard
I was Ni   eye of change
leadress   pathfinder   healer of the breach.

The Surveyor

In memory of Evelyn Tate, 1913 – 1985

The boy knew her
toothless recluse
crouched in that sea desert
castway, survivor of husband,
of lovers, of susu

he travelled with her beneath the surface
of her mind, where covered moon-lit cities lived
carved from the richness of her net of solitude
within the wilderness of her hair, rivers poured
forests of mahogany, blue mahoe and cedar bloomed

she could take flight
borne by the wings of her great skirt
leap from peak to valley
bearing him through caves of silenced memory
through the islands' chain of cauldrons.

he hid when with careless courage
she cracked the riding whip
to bring the flat white lizard
in one blow to death
and exorcized the rapping devils
with country words he couldn't learn

before dawn
the morning after she had died
in dew mist and horse-hooved music,
he heard the flap of skirts and
turning touched her hem

~

she gone.
he, captured by the world
a slave of time
for his living
burned in smoky cities
surveying forests
rivers, seascapes at a distance.

Sometimes, in conversations, her voice
will lead his tongue and she in him
will roll like waves and drums
then there is a wet sound of breathing dreams
still submerged
but growing nearer.

History's Posse:
Family Portraits

Self Portrait

I

In the mirror a white woman peers back at me
droopy cheeks squeezing the corners of an old smile
skin loosened under the chin, jawline eroded,
black frown lines between the brows
as if someone had begun to write something on the face
and had to stop suddenly. Two greenish eyes
lidded with a net of tiny purple veins.
Straight lashes. Coarse skin. Remnants of moles
where a dermatologist left sloppy scars. Turned up nose.
Cheekbones rise stubborn as old hills
in an otherwise unremarkable geology.

II

After years of wishing them cuplike, firm and small,
like the ones in soft porn American pin-ups, I've made peace
with my heavy breasts, their fullness, the large nipples and
resigned myself to carrying their heavy load. Underneath I am
nursing a crop of warts, medals from my forties. The skin round
my strong thighs is dimpled and a green pattern of veins
springs out like a satin-stitched vine on my aunt's tablecloth.

III

These days my body swells
like a volcano before the blood comes.
There is a hot weight inside
where all the ancestors' quarrels
cook down in my shut-pan womb.
In restless dreams, the old mango tree
in Grandma's Hope Road yard is uprooted.
The woman's tongue has fallen in a hurricane.
The poinciana leans on the telephone wires.
Dying vines rope through their limbs in the hard sun.
Or I am standing on the other side of the flooded gully
after Hurricane Flora holding loaves of bread.
But I can't cross the muddy churning water to the others.

All the labour we spent in the yard is in that mud:
the double hibiscus and the desert flower,
the pumpkin vine with her huge offerings,
the ackee tree and the paw paw.
Somebody's cow goes by. A dog.
The bodies of drowned children.
A goat and her kids.

And then fire comes. It cracks and spits.
Its red tongue licks up all I lost —
my mother, my lovers and *compañeras*,
old friends that turned to strangers,
a place I used to call my home.

I am swelling. Waters thicken my body.
I see different countries, in each eye
speak in two languages at once.
I will burst now, songing
like the woman's tongue crisp pod
I will scatter
scatter, survive drought
October floods, the choke of weeds
and shoot out blooms which open
at midnight on the hottest July.

History's Posse

History's Posse

THE FIRST I KNEW MYSELF was in a white house on a hill. It looked out on a bright aqua sea and a smooth palm-lined road below. Orchids bloomed and there were rare birds in the yard. One day I saw a man chopped to death outside the gate. The killers were uniformed. From every finger on their hands a knife blade bloomed. Silver bullets and shark's teeth lined their throats. There were diamond knuckledusters on their fingers.

"Who's that?" I asked my mother as the body twitched to silence in the dirt.

"Sshhh," she said. "That's History's posse come back again. What a crosses come down on me! Don't ask no more. Do, mi baby keep quiet. Get inside and close the door."

Some children were playing in the mud walking barefoot, eating guinep and singing, "What canya do Punchinella little fella? What canya do Punchinella little gal?"

"Let me go and play," I said to Mama. "Hmmph," she said. "Not today. History's posse might be passing by."

"Who is this History?" I asked. "I want to see his face."

"Sshh! Child, nobody looks in History's face. His people are everywhere. He's all around like the air," she whispered. "Do, mi baby, keep quiet. Let's go inside."

"No," I stamped. "If I can't play at least I can watch."

"Come down from there. Is not safe. There are rules, yuh know. Try to make things different and you'll lose everything. That's rule number one."

"Are you my real mother?" I asked her the next day.

"What a crosses this," she said. I asked again, but she shut her mouth and looked far away.

"Where's my real mother then?" and I jooked her hard in her side.

"Alright. Since yuh so fast and so womanish I will tell yuh. Your mother is dead for going gainst History. Come. Close the door and stay inside."

"Where's my father?"

"Don't ask me no more question child. He left yuh this big house to live in. He sends money every month. What more yuh want than that? What a trial, what a cross this child is to bear."

"Where's my father?"

"Alright. Since yuh so inquisitive, since yuh so forceripe, I will tell yuh. Your father is History, himself."

A woman was passing on the road below. She sang:

Peel head John crow sit up a tree top
Pick off di blossom.
Let me hold yuh hand gal.
Let me hold yuh hand.

I thought if I could sing like that, the world would be safe and Mama would laugh and everything would be alright.

Well, I stayed in that house for a time. Every day I practised till I could sing my songs with a voice clear like river water. Mama would smile and rock to the beat. People passing would hear and stand still as ghosts on the road below. But my mind had already gone from that house. Its emptiness cramped me then like a cell. It pressed on my throat like a chain. Only the gardens felt safe to me. I prowled the paths like a cat, tearing out the weeds and chopping back the vines. Night-blooming jasmine scented the air. There was desert flower and there was a cactus that bloomed at midnight. There were bohinia and surprise bougainvillaea.

One night in the rainy season I ran away from the yard, dressed up just like a boy. I hid out my first night in a bus shell, near to a tourist town. My teeth chattered from fear, but I was proud to hell of myself. All night I perched up watching, but in the morning I was fine. I must have got a little too boasty though, for the next night some men stopped me on the road.

"Where yuh going?" they said. "This road not yours to walk. Go home to yuh big yard. That's where yuh belong."

"Tell History for me," I said, "I not playing his game."

They pulled off my disguise then, laughing so hard they could hardly stand up. But they only scratched my throat with the ratchet blade. Blood dulled the knife's silver-edged glint.

"History say yuh can take yuh chances, but yuh can't hide," one said. "Your skin glitters bright in the dark. We can sight yuh anyweh yuh go."

"I'll zip out of it," I said. "There's an opening between my legs." They only laughed more.

Well I did. Unzipped, I rose up flapping, high and cool as a kite. But I had no form. Unnamed, nameless, invisible, I floated over the landscape of burnt cane, over the all-inclusives and their swimming pools, over the markets and the stalls of jerk chicken. I looked down on everything. I was hungry but I couldn't eat. I was tired but I couldn't sleep. I was vulgar abstract. No context at all. It was like being trapped in a dream. "History," I thought, "you win this first round."

A woman was there sweeping the street. She had a cast eye, but her body was wiry and hard. I knew she had courage if that means nothing to lose. "Catch me in a bottle and I'll come down," I entered her vision. "What yuh going gimme?" she said and hissed her teeth like snake.

"I'll give yuh my dreams."

"Dream?" she steuptsed again. "Dream can build house?"

I said "yes."

"Yuh too lie," she laughed, "but yuh funny and I like to laugh."

She brought me down and hid me and I lived in her board house near the train tracks. On her dresser she kept the Bible, a big pink comb and a leaf of aloes. We didn't eat much. I taught her my songs and she showed me tricks I could use in a fight. At night we slept in a bed of rags scented with khus khus, her arm around me like a shield. I called her Vida for she was the first life I knew.

One day, there was money on the counter and fancy linen on the bed. She said, "Yuh mean all this time yuh have yuh big house and yuh don't say not one word. Imagine. I never know is so yuh stay and I struggling to keep body and soul together."

I thought, "time to go."

"Yuh can't just walk out like that," she said. I figured she was History's woman now and we would have to fight. I slipped her through the back, but History's posse was in the yard.

"Dutty gal. Sodomite gal," a red-eye one said. "Yuh notten more than a mule. Get back inside. I'm the Don Gorgan, here. This is my territory. Yuh can't negotiate."

"Slip him like I did show yuh, idiot," Vida shouted.

"Shut up yuh two-mouthed bitch," I screamed, but I was scared to rass. I froze to the spot and the pi-pi ran down my legs. The red-eye one laughed. He pulled out his teeth and scattered them on the ground. They bloomed like the sweet jasmine I'd left behind. I wanted my old house and Mama. I wanted to close the door. I longed for a glimpse of the sea and the white road below.

"Yuh can't even go back to your risto yard. Yuh too soiled with the sex of ole neaga. Yuh can't do notten. Yuh don't have no use to us, wandering like a crazy red cockroach."

I wanted to clothe myself in my songs, wrap myself in a sheath of pure sound. I opened my mouth, but not a single note came out. Not a sound. Silence.

Then a man they said was History himself came in. He was a greyish man in a greyish suit, but I couldn't get a look at his face. I wouldn't know him if I saw him again. The thing is, I couldn't make myself struggle at all. My spirit was nearly gone, yuh hear?

I remember that he said, a lesson is a lesson and if I'd learn mine and do mine I'd be alright. He said, "yuh pass your place, gal."

When I came to I was somewhere dark and stink like a jail. My body was twisted and swollen and it felt hot and cold, hot and cold. "I'll die now," I supposed, "for I'm all alone and I don't even know how to fight. Mama was right. I shouldn't have tried to escape."

I lay there at the curve of a white darkness — in the middle of that hot and cold bleeding. A woman like someone in a dream came in. Maybe I made her up; maybe she was real. I have no memory of how she looked. I only remember the swish of her skirts and that she brought sinkel bible and a cup of something cool to drink.

I said, "Tell History I'll do whatever he wants."

"What yuh want with him again. Yuh don't learn nothing yet?"

"He take away my songs," I muttered hoarse. "I want them back."

She whispered, "Stop sorry for yuhself. If yuh want get out of here, make the sounds like how yuh feel. It won't sound lovely but it will ease yuh heart." And then she left and closed the heavy door.

I cried then, softly at first and then loud and horrible, tearing the night in half. I bawled for my mother who had left me, for my father trapped in his cruelty. I bawled for my fraidy puss Mama. I bawled for the garden swallowed up with bush and weeds. I cried for the blood and the death I had seen. I bawled for my lost songs and for Vida. But most of all I cried for myself. I drank eyewater for breakfast, lunch and dinner. I cussed everything and hit myself against the wall. Sometimes I just stared into the darkness and let the water run down my face. Day followed night while I cried. My tongue stuck to my dry mouth, and my eyes were swollen shut. My heart was locked in an iron grid but it beat slow and stubborn like a repeater drum.

Then one day I saw the sky grow bright, like a pastel pallet outside the bars on the window. It was magenta and grey and blue over the mountains. The crescent moon was watching in the pale sunrise. Mawga dogs barked at the daylight. Between some old newspaper and a rusty tin can, two grass quits did little dances on the ground. There were women selling at the corner and people going up and down. Minibuses were at the bus stop and the ductors in the doorways fought over the fares. The door seemed to open then and a thin bright ledge stretched out. "Go on quick," said the woman's voice. I stepped outside then and stood up straight in the morning dew. I brushed off my old dirty clothes, wiped my face and headed out for the open road.

my mother's last dance

Prelude

First the humming drum and then the solo violin
My mother is beginning her last dance
Deep in the valley of the Rio Nuevo
her first home is now her last.

Reaching up up up, to where the kites are trapped in the wires:
high, high she goes, walking on wires, loosening the children's
kites and the bright colours rain down to open hands like all the
words she thought but never spoke.

And all her past is present
rising on the yard's edges
her faded wedding satin
her tiny sister's hands
her Grandmother Eva sitting
in the same old seat in the old cool shade
Eva's past entwined in the tree limbs
in the voices of the women
who now fill her head.

*My
Mother's
Last Dance*

But yuh see mi trial. Imagine Eva nuh come a work dis morning and mek all di washing come down pon me one.

Yuh nuh hear seh she pregnant?

Cho! Dat a nuh notten.

Dis a nuh any everyday belly. Dis a Ole Massa belly. Nuh di same ole time story. Dem seh Missis find out and hell pop up here last night. It end up dat dem run her.

How she going manage and is five a dem she have?

Hmmph. If a me, him couldn't just get weh so.
Him would haffi pay fah. Small axe fall big tree.

Mother and Child
Bluefields 1890

When Grandma Ames was born, they wrapped her in cotton
and held her out to her mother, who vomited.
Lying back, Eva felt something red and wet
like rage crawling slowly out of her traitorous womb.
Burnt calabash and magnesia, afu yam leaf
and cerasee all betrayed her too when she tried
to dash it way. The violent cramps and the blood
left her weak, but the little something
like a spiteful guinep stain wouldn't come out.
She couldn't face the knife. So half out of defeat,
half out of curiosity, for no other child
of hers had ever been so headstrong
before birth, she went on with the pregnancy.

But every morning she fought that inevitable future
that repetitious legacy of greathouse and canefield,
banding down the tough little belly
winding a sheath of cloth round and round
till her middle looked like a huge bandaged wound.
Then she sat by the door of the little board house
absently embroidering a pair of crazy Mas Corny draws
for a few pence. Her mind a stone, skipped and skipped
the glassy Bluefields bay, then sank,
thankful the voices on the white road were faraway,
thankful that neither her sister nor even her son knew
about the belly. And so could ask no question,

expect no answer. She waited, her mind travelling
the aqua sea to Panama to Cuba, to Costa Rica
while the belly pushed like a bull bucker
against the skin of all her possibilities.

This Sabito Sea gazing. This disillusion.
This disengagement. This ole drunk she married
who did not-a-rass all day, only drink rum
and gamble till him all teef the very weddin ring
off her finger while she was sleeping and,
hallucinating freedom sweet as cane juice, smelling money
rich as the scent of molasses, uselessly use it
to mix his stinking sweat with rum and cards.
And after disappear. Leaving her in the mess
of his sticky dream. Leaving her with the open mouths
of children to hold her there. She had to take
her foot in her hand and walk it
clear to Sav La Mar to beg Parson to find
a little work for her. And she get the job advertise
on the church notice board for the "decent woman
wanted to keep house at Shrewsbury",
(the Haughton estate.) Decent woman. Steuppps

"Yuh should be thankful yuh get the work"
Elfreda said, her godmother who had worked beside
her father and then bought out the dingy
little doctor shop in Great George St.
"If Mr. Man even want a lickle piece, give him.
For is him give yuh roof over yuh head. Yuh can feed
the pickney dem. Yuh is not nobody," she added

self-righteously pouring and stirring the medicine.
"Yuh young and yuh brown. Yuh lucky more than me.
Count your blessing and stop complain." The rat bat
trapped somewhere, wings bound, beat itself over and over
against time's body as it embraced her,
hot breath stirring her hair.

The birth too had the iron will of her pregnancy.
She tried and failed to deliver the child herself.
Then the midwife came. (Just passing and stop
to look in and see how you keeping.) Puff puffing
her disapproval as the pain twisted the unbound bundle.
Eva bore down, teetering on the edge of a precipice
overhanging a wild mud murky sea, anxiety
blinding her remaining will. Out of control. Gone.
So it was a huge relief to her when
looking at the fairskin child, she knew
she didn't have to feed it and stubbornly wouldn't.

Through the clearing sea, face after face came,
women opening and closing their mouths
like fish under water. She, hot enough
not to hear the sound that came and stood up
like a wall all round her, thick and rocky
as those grey stones stacked at the boundaries
of the Shrewsbury cow pasture, said nothing.
She turned up her pupils. Her laboured breathing
caused them to whisper and tiptoe away —
except for Fred her eldest, trapped in his mother's eyeball
and his father's jealousy. His mother's breastpin.

My
Mother's
Last Dance

He took the baby, who beached herself on his hard male breast,
like one a them cotton tree canoe riding the high tide
full of fisherman coming from Pedro Banks
to throw themselves on the womanness of Sabito sand.

He held the screaming child between his mother
and himself, he rocked her, kissed her, bathed her,
oiled her and washed the old cloth she was wrapped in.
It was he who loved her. And they teased him.
called him mamaman, till he hid and did it.
But he never stopped though his mother watched
silently, sullenly, jealously. He suffered her cut-eye
though it hurt him to his heart, but he knew
that the child was a shield against his mother
a shield in which he saw his own reflection and
a chance at something besides raw fish,
salt and drowning. He rocked and sang hymns
to the wrinkled reddish child whose knees
stuck out, whose crawling later on made
a clunking noise like when you draw yam
in crocus bag cross a hill and gully floor.

Eva left to rest found the anger gone, but
not until the stubborn child was a nine-month-old
survivor of malaria and typhoid, did Eva say
"Give me the baby." She took the bad-tempered child,
wanting to win her son from the futures he saw swimming
in the bush baths where his baby sister soaked.
My grandmother didn't scream. She sat on the lap
of the woman she had lain inside for eight months,

absorbed by the long nose, the huge eyes
shadowed and flecked like the full moon and she smiled.

Eva sighed and rocked her, rocked her, rocked her
till her cooing was strong as the child's will to live.
Eva's mahogany arm rested against the infant's yellow sanders
like threads laid out for her rainbow embroidery and
she gazed at herself mirrored in the child's black eyes
thinking how the bloody cord had become a rescue rope
and she gave thanks for the supreme grace of their survival.

My
Mother's
Last Dance

Shame-mi-lady. Shame

I

THEY SAID EVA'S DAUGHTER Ames had a mean mouth.

You might say she looked Indian or clear skin. But whatever she was physically, spiritually she was vex. Vex. Vex. Vex. And she covered the vexation with shame. For vexation itself was a shame — and as they said — especially a shame in a woman. As long as she could remember she had been ashamed. First, there was the memory of being rocked, Sunday visits from her father, games and the things he brought. Then it changed.

A man came one night. Riding a mule. Her sisters ran to him but the man didn't stop. He rode the mule up the steps right inside the house. "Whore gal," he shouted. "Where yuh hidin bacra's bastard?" Cups crumbled under the mule's hoof. Pictures slithered down the wall and crashed as he whipped them.

(She thought, as a stool beside her fell and the blue-bordered cup cracked: "He is shouting because of me.")

Her mother pushed her behind her. There was blood on her hand. Then Meta grabbed her and raced with her out the back door. But she tripped and the man came with the breathing hard mule, Meta threw her. She remembered that forever. Flying through the air, her own scream a raft. She landed in the shoe black, her scream still wrapped round her. Then Fred pulled her by the miraculously unbroken hand and Fred and her sister half-dragged, half-lifted her till they took off again through the back and down the path by the river. Hid her under Miss Kissty's bed.

Hmmmph. Something happen. Little later, they brought her back. The house was a pile of broken egg shells. The place was raw. And after they put her in to sleep, she tek time tiptoe out. Saw her mother, staring at the night watchfully, the curtain hiding her puffy face.

After that everything changed. The Sunday father never came back. Nobody explained a thing. They just kept her in the house, till she took house colour. Till she learned she was different from them. She was not to speak patwa like them. Not to bathe in the river like them. Or go to sea beach like them. Or wander through the pasture like them. Or catch django like them.

They told her, "Do not speak to your father if you see him, unless he speaks first." She didn't ask why. When she saw him coming, her heart beat loudly, but she lowered her eyes and crossed the street. Once she thought she heard him call her. She turned to answer, but he kept going. Not seeing her, his gaze falling beyond her. His kerchief wiping his red face. His voice calling to somebody else. Not her.

He terrorized her dreams. Even so, at night in bed she told herself stories of how her beauty and kindness won her the town's attention, forced his pride. Like a seduced lover he announced at a ball he was her father.

People whispered when they saw her coming along the dust-covered street (Shame-mi-lady. Shame.) The rage she was born with curled inward like a snake.

Shame-mi-lady. Shame
Shame-mi-lady. Shame

And what she learned she taught her daughter.

Shame-mi-lady. Shame
Shame-mi-lady. Shame
Shame-mi-lady. Shame

Come here! Where yuh was?
Yuh was at the river.
If yuh tell me a lie,
I cut yuh tail this morning.

Go for Mr. Alligator
Go for it.
Now! (SLAP)
Where yuh were? (SLAP)
Talk nuh! (SLAP)
Who and you were there?
Don't back answer me! (SLAP)
You and that child from cross the river!
Come back here to me!

How many times I have to tell yuh
don't leave the yard. Yuh hear me?
Yuh too hard ears.
Yuh must know who to mix up with.
STOP RUBBING UP YOURSELF WITH THE PICKNEY CROSS THE RIVER.

Turn round. Stand still.
Let me fix your hair.
I don't know where I get yuh from.
Yuh must be a throw back.
No decent man going want to marry yuh.
Yuh going have to work for yuh living.
You mark my words: yuh better study hard.
Learn yuh lessons. Turn round.

I see it in the paper seh they having a scholarship exam
in Oracabessa next month. They have a scholarship for a girl
to go to the High School in Brown's Town. One so-so scholarship
them have for the whole parish. I sending yuh for the exam. Yuh
better make sure when yuh come home yuh have it in yuh pock-
et. Yuh hear me? Hmmpgh!

Yuh too dark.
Turn round I say.
Little more yuh gwan
till yuh make shame and disgrace come down pon poor me.
At least your hair is little goodish.
I don't know why it won't grow long.
I don't know why God give me a child with hair like yours.
Can't even curl.
Aaay.
After all the prayers I pray.
God knows I try my best.
God knows I try my best.

Transfusion

My mother's mind was cultivated in the walled quadrangle
of a boarding school spliced between market town and
yam hill, pimento, bamboo and Jamaica brahman
in the almost English landscape of St. Ann.

White ladies posted between the breadfruit trees
stood on wooden galleries like stewards
on the margins of "The Negro Question".
They plotted practical methods for cultivating
hybrid orchids and ortaniques and transplanted
scientific dreams of equality deep in the bone
of their brownskinned exceptions.

From the red earth among the orange and
yellow heliconia to the stony
grey of Scotland where she, cap and gowned,
became that better-than-you dark healer,
lady doctor, cutting out cancers blooming like coralilla
easing the coiling vines that block fertility.
Her step heavy on the wards of the Victoria Jubilee Hospital
scattering nurses, summoning those white ladies,
their sarcasm, and their distance, to perform
clinical operations and get them right.

Daddy the Divine

In his shining hour
my English father dropped bombs on Germany
and then retired
to a life of exploration
and eccentricity in the colonies.

When I knew him, he came on Sundays only
and we played under surveillance.
One day, he built a big castle out of sand
and said "I'm going away. Back to England to live."
He gave me two 78 records
"Rip it" up was one. The other was
"Little Darlin Bop bop bopshiwawa
Little Darlin bop bop bopshiwawa
Oh ho where are yoohooooo?"

I didn't cry.
I kissed him on his prickly moustache
and he went away and never came back.

II

In the dead of my desperate nights
he always finds me. Whispers, "don't be afraid of me.
It's your mother's fault you think I'm mad.
You know her version only.
Let me tell you the other side.

They say I lie, I rave, invent things
but I say the truest truths are in my tales.
I speak the spark you need to carry on.
If you don't believe me, ask Parboosingh,
the artist. He knows me.
He'll tell you how I moved his brushes
without touching even one.

All who travel with me know what I can do.
I show them turquoise underwater worlds,
coral laced with pink filigree shells,
fish flashing violets invisible to the eye,
show them the hero in themselves for
I am Dionysus, the god of wine
I am Shiva, the destroyer
I am Shango, the warrior
I am the first white manifestation of Rastafari: (Bull Bay 1949)

Not every manjack can rise to heroic tasks.
Those that try and fail are merely clowns
and their tomfoolery the source
of some damn good belly laughs.
That's why they conspire against me.
That's why they throw me off their front verandahs
drive me out of their yards and rum shops
drug me, malign me, tie me up with rope,
handcuff me, tear me into little pieces
and lock me away.

Come closer. Don't be scared.
I want to tell you something:
They want to murder me.
Oh I know some have to die to resurrect
but it's not me they want to kill.
It is themselves for the absence of poetry
in the smallness of their souls.

Now my own little darling,
is there a Shango or a Shiva in you?"

III

The coroner gave an open verdict
A discrepancy, the letter said,
in the date on the suicide note
and the overdose of drugs and alcohol
might have been accidental.
It was some years
before I learned
he shot himself
through the head.

Wings

Wings carried us to safety — me inside her swimming
blind in the safety of that sac — Wings fragile,
translucent, fine as the small sheets
of membrane that cover the tiny brown cotton seeds
falling softly from trees in the yard, once a year,
the wind taking them up from the dry Liguanea plain
up over the houses and hills then floating them
down slowly to the green to grow.

(After his breakdown and hospitalization/ my husband
referred constantly to my efforts to help him get well
with resentment and mistrust/ abusing me far into the
night/ about April he took great exception to the
irregularity of my work hours due to my medical
practice/ we had several quarrels about this/ one
night after such a quarrel my husband struck me again
and again in the face/ he took away my car keys
saying if I couldn't guarantee my hour of return he
would stop me going to the hospital at all)

The womb waters must have been choppy or rough,
but the wings were threaded with filaments of magenta and indigo,
emerald and silver, and they never broke no matter how high
the cobalt waves, how cold the northern sea

till they went and came back from Montreal and earthed me
finally in the brown ground of the house my Grampa
bought Grandma on Hope Road, his line so long,
his generation so plentiful, their muscled bodies
rippling out of the islands dark rock like Michelangelo's incomplete
carvings, their flesh patterned with scars from treadmill, from fire,
survivors of the future as if they were sparks
from his uncle's blacksmith forge on Bluefields beach.
Grandma Gokul and Grandma Forrest breaking, shovelling,
and working the tough red earth till it became graceful spun silver
aluminium wings and they painted Pan American Airlines flight 402
on the side and carried us to icy Montreal.

> (it was hard, sleeping on those strangers' couch
> so cold so cold I froze your nose/ and you were a
> such a tiny colicky baby/ you cried and cried/ I was
> frightened/ alone/ Once you cried for
> six hours straight/ I was afraid they'd put us
> out/ Didn't know what to do/ Didn't know who to ask
> I opened the window of the apartment/ held you
> over the snow so they wouldn't hear your screams)

*My
Mother's
Last Dance*

The shock recedes like water on hot sand.
Only little bubbles pop up now and again,
the Armageddon sound is dying like the plane's
engines slowing down, propellers becoming visible again
and the world present again, though strangely white

And me pushing my way out in that space
between the old colony, northern first nation,
the old imperialists, and the new. The subversive
gesture of living, the disorder of desire
written only on that infant's open mouth
sucking sucking against the threat of death
between the imprint of history in my face
and the beating of her heart against my ear.

Grandma Ames Prays
for Her Children

Have mercy on me, Lord for I am
One foot in the grave and one out.
Still here for what reason I don't know
For me no have no use again
Can't bake again; can't sew again.
Son dead, and Winsome dead
and Joyce bring down shame and disgrace
pon poor me with that man till they carry
the divorce clear to *The Evening Star.*

(If I was ever to tell you, Lord,
what that man do me, the words he use ....
but I would never repeat it
before your glorious majesty, Lord
so I just keep it in my heart. But what
hurt me, more than all is how a man
who speak so well and look so good
could be so wicked, and how he tell me
his nastiness in the perfect Queen's English
that poor me can't even speak.)

That's why I tell those children be careful
who you keep as friend. Play with Puppy,
Puppy lick yuh mouth. Lie with dog yuh rise with flea.
And Everton from ever since only looking
for the blackest child to carry home from school.
Instead of looking up, he only looking down.
And the whole a dem so hard-ears
I don't know why I bother waste my breath.

I sounding constant warning:
Any minute disaster can strike
Be on your guard.
For living is like house cleaning
As fast as you clean out the place,
somebody nasty it up again.

Pneumonia

The scent of oranges
and half a dozen suns
at the bottom of the iron bed
blaze up at me
where I am lying
in a blue place
near the ceiling
freed from my hot feverish body
gone from the kas kas
and cuss cuss
of the house on Hope Road
where safety is fragile
as a banana leaf,
torn easy as the net over my crib
sliced like the woman who wept
as my mother stitched
her flesh one Sunday morning,
the warm blood running
down the green verandah tiles

"I bring
ortaniques for you"
my mother's cool presence
is rare, but now her heavy steps
drum closer echoing
on the polished pitch pine floor

the ortaniques in
her big hands
shine up at me
where I am looking
down at my child's body
cool, limp in the damp sheets,
my mother's face pinched
her big fierce eyes shrunken from worry.
My mother is a huge cloud.

The
orange glow
the sweet citrus smell dripping
from the living fruit
are in her fingers.
I turn
open my eyes
into her gaze
stretch out to touch the suns
chose to live, to see my mother's smile.

Swimming Lesson

My mother is teaching me to swim
staying afloat in the clear aqua
is a struggle for her   she wants me
to be better than her   stirs up
the sand when she goes   darkens
the clear and swims like one a them trapped
blue marlin butting and butting my uncle's boat
thrashing the line of the Sunday deep sea killers
trawling in the blood past the reef
one hand on their rods, the other on their Chivas Regal.

In the water where she can stand
she says   swim to me now
and I begin the crossing
clumsy   laborious   spluttering
banging my little bones
the disparate pieces of arm
leg   shoulder   against the angles
of the deep water, pausing
gulping between splattering on
longing to reach her body's harbour.

As I am about to reach, to rest
"Come on, come come come man," she laughs
and moves further off again
I am tired. Kicking angry. Shicoom. Shicoom.
glugging up through the bubbles
the hard blue for air and the misty sands
blur the water   so I never reach the end
this homeless groundless body
struggling not to fight
the water   not to thrash
to flash streamlined like the conquering
trawler gliding into port.

Westmoreland 1962

One time
she let me come. It was independence week.
("Yuh growing up" my cousin said)
only once a year they went there.
I was twelve. My mother said "No school today.
It's time you learned Westmoreland."
We drove for hours. The medicine bag
and tins of food rattled at my feet. Under
the bamboo arches we ate roast yam and salt fish,
a man showered naked at a standpipe by the sea
(Jackie covered my eyes and giggled.)
A herd of cows blocked a truck,
an old man played a comb outside a shop
where my uncle stopped to ask the way.
A higgler went the other way on a donkey,
her feet jerked and dragged in the dust.

By a tree stump we turned off. Guinea grass
licked the wheels of the car. There was no sign
or road or track. Breadfruit leaves scalloped
edges off the sky. Black pods of orange poinciana
clanged on the roof top of the car. The mountains
rose smooth as the breasts of a woman,
trapping the early evening smoke.
scent of cedar and eucalyptus
between the earth and air.
Birds crossed the five o'clock sky.

*My
Mother's
Last Dance*

Rounding a curve in the pasture
the old great house appeared like a mirage.
abandoned/burnt/perfectly preserved in creepers
not even a squatter inside, the tables set, in the amber
sunset (like that house preserved in Cuba) the stuffing hung
from the seat of a broken chair, birds squeaked
in disintegrating lattice. And the spaces round it.
Holes. The holes filled with nothing.
Grey rock foundations solid in the black earth.
Into the bush again and through the plantain
and wild banana, the root embroidered walk
behind somebody's yard, to the wood shack.
(Mummy said "Bring the bag")

In the clearing by her board kitchen
Aunt Lilly sat one pale hand on a rust-streaked cutlass.
The blade poised on the firewood, the other arm raised high
"Yuh come? Alleluia, Praise the Lord," she sang,
her nails shining in the sun.
(Aunt Lilly did it with a cripple
when she was too young. A fiddler.
He gave her music lessons.
That's why yuh to mind yuhself
and don't make no boy trouble yuh.
My cousin whispered on and on.)

"Let I take yuh inside" she smiled and said.
Rotting linoleum and floorboard,
her son a bent chassis
of bones/holes/blisters.

"That's Rick" she smiled. "No mind darling;
the journey upset yuh stomach.
I going boil some mint tea for yuh. I know."
"Say good evening," my mother commanded.
"I don't know why yuh bother come," Rick muttered
"Yuh should carry me and Mama to Kingston
long time. But it don't suit yuh.
Now yuh turn big shot yuh prefer
hide us away uppa mountain."

(Don't wee wee here,
unless yuh do it in the bush.
The pit toilet smell too bad.
And it have one hell of a green lizard
on the window. Wait till we get to Sav, Jackie said)

Here are the pills and the injections.
The bedclothes you wanted and the new nighty
and new panty and slippers.
Here are towels, tins of bully beef and mackerel.
Here is a transistor radio. Here are batteries
A flashlight. And matches for the fire
Here is the kerosene oil
("Take yuh hand from yuh mouth," Jackie said.
"Twelve years old. Behave.")

Behind in the hill
board houses cotched on stones
staggered from rock to rock.
No light and a rough black cloth
dropped hard on the still breathing landscape.
Till moonrise in the darkness only peeniewallies
blinked on/off/on/off like Christmas in the dry hills.

On the way down, my mother said
"You mean is only here people
still can't own land?
Nothing's changed.
O my God in forty years
nothing's changed."

Aux Leon Women

Before the sunlight
splits the dry rock
their eyes open
on coarse board walls and
guttered
government
land

mind set begins
with stumbling over
a sleeping child
an animal immobile.

"catch up the fire/ scrape and grate the cassava/ carry the water
(uphill)/ boil the tea/ the toloma/ beat the castor oil seeds/ wash
clothes/ nurse baby/ soothe old lady/ weed garden/
chop banana/ load banana/ carry it down the stony road/
Un cadeau pour Monsieur Geese."
la lin coowee, coowee
la solei joo baway
(the moon runs
it runs
till the sun
catches it)
"how much are the bananas today?/ the housewife said
unbuttoning her coat/ laying down her string bag in the
Islington shop/ hurry up there/ don't have all day/ she added

My
Mother's
Last Dance

himself will be home soon and the tea not ready/ nothing
changes/ only the prices rise/ Gimme a dozen a them/ bruised
lot you got here today"
la lin coowee, coowee
la solei joo baway
(the moon runs
it runs
till the sun
catches it)
scrape/boil/beat
"sleep baby sleep
father working far away
he give me something   i take it
he give me nothing   i take it"

Aux Leon women
This morning
when the sunlight strikes
the rock
Let us sweep that old yard clean.
Let us beat our quarrels into one voice
with the rhythm of the hardwood pestle.
Let us light our fires on this hillside
so all the islands will see
this labour is not free.
Let us burn the sweet wood
for its scent with fill the nostrils
of the blind and deaf.

listen
(La solei coowee coowee
la lin joo baway)
The stroke of a cutlass in water has no meaning
(La solei coowee coowee
la lin joo baway)

Listen, a song —
a song is beginning
right here
among us.

(Note: Aux Leon is a small community in St. Lucia, situated near Dennery on the eastern side of the island and created by squatters on the high and rocky back-lands of an old estate.)

Grandma Ames Prays for Her Children Again

I

Is me same ole sinner, Massa God
come to tell yuh seh dolly house mash up again
This second husband walk out and leave Joyce
No word. No war. Just ups and gone
See yah Lord, I can barely repeat all what I hear
that mongoose-face brown man carrying on
since him gone back to him mountain.
He have one two three cars up there
and I hear every morning him carry up
one of the little white doctor
from the university in the Rover and
them do whatsoever them waan do.
Lunch time him carry her down in the Jaguar.
In the evening he carry up a little turn colour nurse
and when him done with her him carry her down
in the Austin. Little more yuh see him
come with a half-chinese one.
Whentime he finish with she
them tek time and go down in the beforeday
so nobody can't see them to talk.
Hmmph.

Call himself doctor.
Him is notten but a ragin ramgoat.

Don't want no doctor like that
put him hand pon me at all tall.
Him too nasty

Have mercy on Joyce
(even though is she wrong to take up with him)
for she is both mother and father

The nice nurse passing
her room on Wednesday
just happen to look in on her
and find her travelling.
One of them had to run
and throw water on her,
massage her heart
while the other one was there
calling her to come back
She answered quite
at Death's door.

Lord, she is drifting, drifting
something like the ember gone out of her —
a lost look in her eyes
Her hands cold as ice all the while.

Is that fool fool idiot
call imself doctor
nearly kill her with cure.
I don't want no doctor like that
to put im hand pon me at all tall

My
Mother's
Last Dance

My Joyce is a physician, Lord.
Give her the grace to heal herself.
Release her from the pain.
Bathe her in your cool water
Ease her heart and soul.

II

Last but not least Lord
Have mercy on Everton
for he is carrying down my name
with the whole heap a woman and pickney
inside and out. I wouldn't say bastard Lord
for I can't stand the word,
but when all is said and done that is what they are.
After I bring him come and him see poor me
a trying soul, trying to teach them to hold up them head
for I don't want nobody point no finger at me,
seh "See there" — after all that — he still gone back
gone do the self same thing again.

Merciful Father! Then is so History going go on
repeat itself. Das why Lord, I wouldn't
let none of the unlawful children in the house.
Just as I couldn't go in my father house
(never would I dream of it)
None of them not coming in here.
They must stay far and learn like how I learn
for who can't hear must feel.

All the same Lord he is my first born, my prodigal
Old time people say when ramgoat foot bruck
him find him massa door.
Lead him to your door

For Lord when I think of all that pass
how Son just dead so
how we had to take all what breeze never blow down
and all what never bear yet to pay the debt,
how we end up with empty hands
When I think of these things Lord
Cold sweat wash me. Bad feeling tek me
and my head just spinning spinning spinning.

Yuh can do something good today,
but tomorrow trouble only set up like rain.
Disaster always lurking
and a crowd of ragamuffin waiting to see it lick
to pass remarks, tell story bout yuh
and take yuh name spread table cloth.
The same ole hypocrite that eggs up today
bring yuh down with dem carry-go-bring-come tomorrow
Yuh can't give them not even an excuse to chat yuh
For them born red-eye and grudgeful.
Why Lord? Why no matter how yuh try
breeze always blow down the crop.
Why is it that in the morning
yuh fresh and blooming and in the evening
yuh wither away?

*My
Mother's
Last Dance*

Disputed Truths

Charming! Charming stories!
Except it's all a lie.
And you know it.
Grandma never spoke patwa
and you know it.
Why do you have to keep on
calling your mother
a brown woman?
And she encourages you

I'll never forget that day
at the hospital in Toronto
The doctor asked her
if her skin was that way naturally
or if it's the disease.
The way she rocksed him off
the poor man just shrivelled up.

Nobody would know.
But you have to keep on bringing it up!
At every turn "Brown this! Brown that!"
Who cares! Who gives a goddamn?
Nobody would notice.
But you have it
like some ole cross to bear
You are just obsessed with race.

You just want to be black.
That's all.

Separation Poems

Cloud

Yuh better mind what yuh tell my mother
for my mother is a huge cloud.
Her shadow hangs over Liguanea.
If yuh trouble her,
she will lash yuh with rain
and hard gulping breezes will blow yuh weh.
The dry gully will swell suddenly thick with mud
and the mangrove swamp overflow.

Sometimes she sets up in silence for days
her face purple with rage
dust covers everything
in the still stubborn heat
day after day yuh move in slow motion.
Yuh cyaan do no work,
Yuh pray for rain's release.
Long after, she opens up and pours.
Lightning is her lover,
and Thunder her friend.

Take care. Watch them from far
when I see her coming
I get ready.

I batten down
and I take shelter
yuh hear that sound on the roof
yuh hear that yakata yakata
like a vex spirit stoning the roof?
Is her. She coming.
Little more she will walk
right into this little house
and blow off the roof clean clean.
She nah jestor.
She will sound the heart,
investigate the brain,
the womb, for signs of rebellion.
If she finds anything out of order
she will cut the growth no matter the blood
and diagnose a dose of bitter gall.

II

Amputation
For Two Voices

MOTHER
Once my daughter's heart beat in my body.
Now she is a monster and she chews on my aorta.

DAUGHTER
My mother and I do not communicate.

MOTHER
She says that with my love I suffocate.

DAUGHTER
I said Mom go find yourself a man.
Your needs are choking me.

MOTHER
As if the cord round her neck was never cut
and she has to bite through it again and again.

DAUGHTER
When I was little she wasn't there.
Never had the time,
Now its too late, she's always around.

MOTHER
Formed by all I fought so hard to earn
she styles herself the opposite of me,
says she's shamed by privilege.

DAUGHTER
Decked in diamonds and raw silk suits
her smug friends drive their Mercedes Benz
through the avenues lined with shacks.

MOTHER
The little boonoonoonos who cried
when I went back to work in the afternoon
has become Lady Bountiful of the suffering masses.

DAUGHTER
She doesn't like my friends — wrong class.

MOTHER
Cold, white
invulnerable as alabaster,
patronizing the impoverished
with visions of upliftment
handing down writs of judgement
on the colonized bourgeois — like me.

DAUGHTER
Wrong colour too.
But she would never say that out loud.
And she's the one who said she couldn't go
to the U.S with me when I was little.
Said they'd put me in the bus for whites
and her in the one for coloureds

MOTHER
Damns our desires as our chains.

DAUGHTER
Guess who was in the communist party at University?
You got it. Now, ask her what colour she is.
She can't say it. Afraid to say it.
had to go to North America to find out.

MOTHER
Denounces my taste for whiskey
and French perfume is justice' graveyard.

DAUGHTER
Their tastes for foreign luxuries drain the country dry.

MOTHER
When I see her coming
I have to take a valium.
I just start to tremble all over.

DAUGHTER
I'm ashamed.

MOTHER
There's no mercy in her strategies.
No loving in her actions.
Doesn't believe in private property, she says
but Truth belongs to her alone.
Woebetide the ones who dare to differ.
Her words may be new: her tone is old,
arrogant as a busha with a worker in the field,
righteous as a missionary inoculated with God's will.

DAUGHTER
Home is supposed to be a place where you belong,
But I'm always out of place here.

MOTHER
Each syllable slices deep
beneath the skin
threatening with amputation all contaminated.

Both
Once our hearts beat in one body,

MOTHER
Now this strange white fruit has burst from my flesh.

BOTH
The more she turns her searchlight on me,
the more I want to leave my body
on the operating table, and fly away.

III

My Mother's Prophecy

Everything you have, you will lose.
Those comrades singing strident lovesongs
will disappear, water heated to steam.
That redemptive work you think so crucial
it will disintegrate — like so much vanity,
the truths behind it proven partial or complete lies.

The body you were born in will crumble
like old bread piece by piece;
ambivalent, without entry point
your spirit will split between orthodoxies,
angry at the world for all you cannot be,
for the loss of mother, baby, lover, home,
for the labour you laughed at,
the gesture of your casual cruelty,
the privilege you never questioned,
the rights you never exercised
for being late too often or too early,
too strong/ too weak
for being unaware of who you were.

Love isn't what you thought.
Its memory's dust, stale quarrels
the eternally rebellious desire
for the other side.

THE ARCHANGEL

WHEN THE CAR HIT THE IRON PIPE holding aloft the sign at the crossroads, she saw a dark shape at the edges of her vision. She scolded herself as the car that had hit her flashed and zoomed away out of sight toward St. Thomas. "That's what you get for making house calls in this day and age."

And the angel with the large wings who had been there all along waiting to open them, to dip and sway, emerged from the flash, fluttered and cooed like the sisters at Mother Henry's yard in Jones Town and eased her against that ice-cold bosom. At that moment her life seemed to her only the dull pink of the blotting paper given out at St. Hilda's Diocesan High School on Monday mornings, the dull pink of the photographs of a cell she customarily surveyed at office. Then the blotting paper absorbed something red from the outer edges in.

She looked at the circle of faces gathered over her as she lay in the wrecked Honda Civic. She blinked back the red and said "I have fractured a hip."

When a man looked sceptical, she informed him that she was a physician. And if he knew what that meant, he would realize she knew what she was talking about and call this number immediately to tell her patient she had been unavoidably detained and notify her daughter to come at once to the roundabout at Harbour View.

Other faces came then. Familiar faces, but hazy. All was a bright redness. Then dark.

II

It comes softly
from the spine, through the blood
drums rising at a kumina
rising, rising, then the cutting breaks.
Cut. Cut. Cut. Cut

Yes   balance youself between the rhythm
hold to that other self like a piece of bamboo
in big sea   then   the sheets of water lick you
lick you lick you   turn the raft a weapon gainst you
drive it through the spine
chip. chip. chipping bone

A bulldozer smashes the boarded up shacks
marking the trail of where you have been
1939 with your father on deck the banana boat
en route to England colliding with 1976
"socialism is love" rally; with that Saturday
in '46 when Bellevue strikers and police clashed,
and at Kingston Public Hospital
the male doctors had a meeting to discuss
"what's to be done" while downstairs
you worked the wounded with the nurses,
and the puppy at Rock Hall disappearing under the massive
boogoodum of the flat steel bearing down
on the face of your daughter the day she married that American.

Thin tiny hairlike roots of your life
dark light under a microscope the solid bright
merciless blue of the sky uninterrupted
stretching blankly nothingly on

Bulldozer come again
blade power open remembrance's shack
smash the last egg shell round
the wriggling montage of faces.
Fingertips calling those
you tried hardest to forget
wizened ancients thought dead
bubble up like drowning things
in their pitchy patchy scrapsy clothes
dressed as people once feared or
heard of but never really known

Bulldozer scooping again
(Call to the angel there, do. Call s/he. call s/he
have mercy. Have mercy. Lord have mercy)
they rise up from the blue darkness
noiselessly, steppin, steppin
to a mix up of mento or waltz or
tambo or dub. Open mouths grin holding
small heaps of things from their time and place,
shack-shacks, mouths of blood

You had imagined dying a soft harmonious chord
which enveloped pain as quietly as you once
went into the still sea at dawn

for a constitutional bath.
Now dying is a crowd of ragamuffin, stink
with a scent of flesh fired on the bone,
of infected gashes from clashes between Tivoli and Jungle
from yaws and chiga, choleric retching
a stone-throwing crowd like those unseen ones
who stoned your mother from her Orange Hill house.

III

you have worked
48–72 hours at a stretch
sleepless night on day on night
you have worked to develop a gaze
which sees beyond the surface of
the flesh you examine spread on the steel table
you have endured the physical abuse to the healer's body
delivering, suturing, scrubbing, stitching
injecting, lancing, blood on the white
boot beneath the green gown night after night
dying for sleep collapsing cracking open your skull
on the door of the operating theatre.
And what emerged?

Give account. Did it work?
You have not healed with your medicine
the wounds of centuries' habitual cruelty.
Embalmed in your body shut tight
locked up are the things
you could not fix or face.
And so they are liberated now.

IV

And that humming in the shadows like doves
funny how comforting those songs are
I try to hum along with tunes I heard before,
but cannot remember singing ever
though now I hear the words

Fly away home to Zion
Fly away home
One bright morning
when my work is over
gonna fly away home.

Fallen Angel

Doc, yuh fraid a fallen angel?
Yuh have fallen Angel go all bout
And look for people pickney to carry dem weh.
Yuh see whentime you read it inna
Star seh stranger come in a district
And lickle more a pickney disappear?
Is Fallen Angel carry dem way
Fallen Angel love sweetie,
bulla cake or Bustamante backbone
and especially paradise plum.

I nurse one ole teacher fi a year,
she trouble wid sugar.
Dem chop off one a di foot dem
and mi nurse her gwan
till di next foot start give trouble
and lickle more she dead.

And I nurse one ole judge —
Sir sinting warranadda —
him trouble wid him heart.
Night time when di chest tek him
bray like Jackass.

And mi nurse him gwan
till late one night it start on him
and me go fi lickle water to give him
By the time me reach back
mi find him stone cold dead.

And I nurse a Mrs. Hanna till she dead
And Mr. Collymore till him dead
and den I nurse him wife, but she never live long neither
And now I nursing you.
I see one cake in di kitchen Doc.
Please if I can take a lickle piece?

A Place Called Home

my mother is dying
each day a piece of her brain goes away
where does it go?
where will I look for it? in the navy blue sky dark
and tight as my aunt's secretary's skirt/ in the holes
the stars leave on the sky spread/ under the mango tree
cool shade/ or the yellow folds of ackee drying on the concrete
step/ between the chip chip chip of the stones she laid on my
grandmother's land to make a drive
to the place
called
home?

the wings of the northbound aeroplane
slice the hard cloud/ the earplugged muzak's
sneaky messages of styrofoam love ooooe over
the pale greyscapes of icy whiteness.
where? where will I look?
in the long silent fall from the height of this plane
to the blank face of the antiseptic immigration man
coarse hands rummaging through the fragments of mourning
in my old grip/ the hospital's glinting
steel bedside/ computers bleep bleeping
measures of cell, fluid, element and marrow/
the small dark hand on the white sheet's edge

who will I be at the end of these endings?
scraps of me buried in the sheaths of brown
skin wound round the cracked hollow bone
chopped up, upsidedown like Tom Cringle's
Giant Cotton Tree after the bulldozers,
roots bleeding invisible blood into the bright day,
all the ghosts homeless.

O my little nation: my country you are unmapped.

Dinner at the Apartment in Toronto

Silence
is the web encircling us,
noisy as the clanging of washed pots
or the bawling of a cow butchered in the hills.

Discharged from hospital you are sitting
on a couch in a highrise in Toronto.
I sit resentfully opposite looking at you
locked, like Frida Kahlo, in your iron spinal brace
the plastic clasp cutting through the thin flesh
covering your heart. Through the glass
a white sheet covers the city's winter body.

I have stopped work and come here to take care of you.
You're glad I'm here. You want me with you.
I want to get away.   You smile at me.   You plan dinner.
You make dinner.   For though I know I should
I am used to the habit of your taking charge,
accustomed to deferring to your power,
We sit at the table set for the dinner rite
and chew chicken, rice and the obligatory salad in silence.

You have shrunk seven inches in two months since your spine collapsed.
Your ribs splinter each time you stretch.
You never complain, never speak of death or the God you pray to
though the invocation of heavenly intervention is evident
in the tracts from "Unity" and "The Daily Word" beside your bed.

Your disease has rotted my soldier crab's shell
and I am shocked to want what I have condemned.
I inventory my could-have-beens:
a gun toting stockbroking BMW driving husband,
a four bedroom house in Norbrook with two starched helpers,
a gardener, security guard. A proper job. And vicious dogs.
What else? A gate that throws it's arms open at one touch
of my manicured finger to the remote. A flat for you
to live in, devoted grandchildren and a nurse.
These things will never be. This is the end of that,
and I swallow a piece of lettuce and tomato.

You were as I was always told, an anomaly in your time
a woman doctor, single mother, single island scholar,
singular educated woman of colour. Now you are counting
all you were not, as you swallow the rice grains
I see you examining the failed marriages
the effort not to be so distant, to express yourself,
to be ordinary, a middle class woman with a home,
a nuclear family, a love of gossip or dancing,
a wife who tolerates a womanizing husband for the sake of three
children, who sublimates humiliation in church work perhaps,
or embroiders in an armchair by a window.
Those discarded choices have long been dumped or burned.

We have only what has been: the silence and
the loud words thrown like cutlasses across the yard
the jealousies, each other's oppositions,
stalemates and the unresolved differences,
the secrets — shards enmeshed in the web
encircling us — these discontinuities of love.
Dinner is over. We are clearing the table now.

Transfusion 1989

My mother's mind was cultivated in the walled quadrangle
of a boarding school spliced between market town and
yam hill, pimento, bamboo and Jamaica brahman
in the almost English landscape of St. Ann.

White ladies posted between the breadfruit trees
stood on wooden galleries like stewards
on the margins of "The Negro Question".
They plotted practical methods for cultivating
hybrid orchids and ortaniques and transplanted
scientific dreams of equality deep in the bone
of their brownskinned exceptions.

From the red earth among the orange and
yellow heliconia to the stony
grey of Scotland where she, cap and gowned,
became that better-than-you dark healer,
lady doctor, cutting out cancers blooming like coralilla
easing the coiling vines that block fertility.
Her step heavy on the wards of the Victoria Jubilee Hospital
scattering nurses, summoning those white ladies,
their sarcasm, and their distance, to perform
clinical operations and get them right.

Now, in the marrow of her bones her disease
has ripened. Her hands that once cut
living children from the wombs of the dead

My
Mother's
Last Dance

are scabby and shaky, her fingers tough like
ginger root and just as numb. She cannot make
haemoglobin and depends on imports of packed red cells.

Each week she receives the blood of a stranger,
given for her in the old blood bank behind the cemetery
where the street people live in the old mausoleum
and the gun fights rage between the dons.
A baby father's blood, a gunman's blood
The blood of a security guard
The blood of a higgler who trades food in Haiti
The blood of a whore who works the Terra Nova strip
The blood of an old teacher.

Her mind is changed:
she speaks now of the need for Anansi,
the impossibility of survival
by politeness in these times.
And she is not the same:

The gunman is there on guard.
The baby father is nursing his child.
The higgler is counting her change,
hiding it deep between her breasts.
The prostitute is feeding her children.
The school teacher is transforming lesson.

And every night she presses a needle like a nipple
into the skin and the needle is attached to a plastic mouth
like a child's that sucks and sucks

the iron impurities out
and spits them away to the ground.

Subcutaneously begins this exchange of fluids,
of haemoglobin and ferritin, her past
holding their futures, their futures holding
her past and the old brown skin transparent and thin
as the cellophane membrane round the bohinia seed,
is alive and red as the impoverished provision grounds
of St. Ann burnished with an imponderable residue of iron.

The Ambulance

THE AMBULANCE COMES. It is an old thing that looks like a fat metal lizard. It lumbers slowly to a stop as if it has heart disease. Two men come into the house. "Oh my," says Mr. Williams, the older of the two men, "imagine is Doc sick. I never think Doc could sick. From I know her, all when she used to work down a Public, she never sick. Good day Doc," he says going to the bedside, "is a shame to see you so sick when you do so much for so many. Allow me please to say a word of prayer."

Doc feels flattered, for she nods, almost smiles. "Let us pray." We stop in the midst of whatever we are doing. Putting a towel into a bag. Searching for a nightgown. Miss G. who has been pouring out a cup of tea, pours it back into the thermos and clasps her hands. The rest of us bow our heads and shut our eyes. He puts one hand on Doc's head and the other on her hand. "O Lord I am begging you to take this child in charge. I am praying God that you will be the doctor in this operation. I am calling on you to heal her Lord." I open my eyes. The prayer is going to be one of those long ones. "Bow yuh head and close yuh eyes," whispers Miss G. "At least yuh going learn to pray."

They carry her downstairs on a chair. She wants to walk but we won't let her try. She refuses to go on a stretcher. Miss G. goes with her into the ambulance. I watch them go, prepared to follow in the car. Mr. Williams slams his door and ... "Crrups" goes the key. Nothing happens.

"Crrrrups." Still nothing.

A third more deliberate, "Crrrrrrrups."

Mr. Williams sends the other man to open the bonnet. He opens the huge old shrieking lid, studies the engine and knocks something. Finally, he shouts, " Alright. Try her now." Again nothing.

Miss G. comes out of the ambulance. They confer by the left headlamp. "Yuh have any jumper cables?" asks Mr. Williams. Miss G. sucks her teeth. "Yuh no supposed to ask fi dat. Suppose him did have heart attack? Him would a dead already."

"Yuh see Miss," says Mr. Williams to me (ignoring Miss G.), "it really need a new ambulance. Dis old one hardly have any use. But we haffi try a ting. And all yuh try, dem still a undermine yuh." Here he pauses and gives Miss G. a mild cut-eye. "Ah cyaan keep a pair a cables, ah tell yuh. As fast as ah buy a pair dem teef it out. Dem teef di last cables from three month a back and all di requisition I requisition, dem don't pay me no mind."

I look for jumper cables in the trunk of my mother's car. There are none. Mr. Williams looks suddenly weary. He goes to the back of the vehicle. He says something to Doc, and then summons our little group again.

"Yuh will haffi push," he informs us, with no show of fear. Miss G. laughs mockingly, kisses her teeth more loudly.

"But Jesus Christ. Anybody ever see my trial. MAC!" she shouts for the watchman from Arafat's Guest House next door. "COME QUICK! DI GOVERNMENT EMERGENCY AMBULANCE WANT TO PUSH."

MacMillan, the security guard at Arafat's Guest House jumps the fence and comes. We remove Doc from the back to lighten the load and put her under the overhang of the roof. Then we line up behind the van and push. The enormous lizard-like vehicle hardly moves at first and then picks up speed as it hits a brief incline on the driveway. "Clutch it! Clutch it!" shouts Mac.

"What di hell yuh think me a do," shouts back Mr. Williams as the ambulance lurches and hiccoughs and finally comes to a full silent stop by the gate, where the main road traffic streams by indifferently. We lean on the bonnet of the vehicle and pant.

"Come we try it one more time," Mac says. We agree. Mr. Williams comes out and gives us instructions about how we are to push, when to pick up speed, who should stand where, etcetera, etcetera. Two boys selling newspapers, at the corner join the group and Mr. Williams places them between Miss G. and me. A woman selling cigarettes at a makeshift table calls encouraging phrases and asks "Who inside?" and "What do him?" A man who had been waiting at the ruined bus stop across the street also comes. He is put beside Mac at the back. Off we go again down Hope Road. Pushing the empty ambulance past the disconnected traffic lights, past the Governor General's residence, where a policeman standing at the guard box is reading the newspaper, past the roofless church, past the bent rows of electric wires, past the zinc lying on the bankside, finally coming to rest in front of the bent zigzagging fence outside the Office of the Prime Minister. That is where we give up.

When we get back, without the ambulance, Doc has moved herself from the stretcher and has propped herself up in the car. "The state of the health service may be bad, but you don't have to turn it into a poppy show." We drive to the hospital in silence.

My Mother's Last Dance

FIRST, THE HUMMING DRUM and then the solo violin.

My mother is beginning her last dance, deep in the valley of the Rio Nuevo, her first home is now her last. Reaching up up up to where the kites are trapped in the wires: high high she goes walking on wires, loosening the children's kites and bright colours rain down to open hands, like all the words she thought but never spoke.

Then the Don, Death, arrives in a big old Benz. He unfolds his huge height like a long ribbon from the car. His legs are sharp stilts, and in his white gloved hand is a silver capped walking stick. His dark glasses are one-way mirrors. Guns bulge beneath his pin-striped long-tailed coat. He looks at the old watch at the end of a long gold chain on his belly and he flashes his gold-teeth smile, crooks his finger at my Ma and waits. He stands at one end of the swinging bridge. I am at the other. He doesn't have to say stop tapping my wires. The last duel has begun.

My brown mother, the colonized, is doing ballet in the tops of the bamboo clumps, on the edges of the remains of her father's pimento and banana ground. A boy shouts "Get flat" and people get down in the bush, ready for the shots to start. She turns to me where I am standing shrunken into the old board of the bridge and she shows me how long she has been there, loving deep in the black black soil between the rocks, where Mammy Eva took her to bathe, at Oracabessa at the river mouth where they raced on mule-back before there were hotels on the bright sands. And Death has manners, for he backs off and leans up gainst a tree. She shows me again the place where the bones of the ancestors are buried under the old guango tree.

Then she comes back to me at the swinging bridge and says, "Now you must learn to cross." But the height makes my eyes turn and there is nothing to hold on to for the rope rails are rotten and the old board slats are rotten from rain and chi chi. There are holes where you should walk and through the holes I see the foaming white water and the slippery green stones like knives beneath the surface.

My mother says, "It is the only road left. We must cross." Across the bridge Death is pacing, crushing the leaf of life and the baby's breath fern with his pointed feet. Old friends leave one by one. They not staying for this. The sun grows hard and gold.

My mother takes my hand and *abracadabra* I am little again and we are hop-scotching across the bridge one foot at a time. I see she has picked up her old black medicine bag, the one like a grip with a hundred tiny drawers. It's big and bufuto and it weighs so heavy now, she cannot manage it at all. I know it will drop and pull her down into the river water. I know she wants me to take the bag, with its medicines and injections, its rusting stethoscopes and the old silver boxes for sterilized things. "Again?" I say for I know the bag. It is an old argument we have. "It don't have no use to me," I say. "And is you cause it".

She leans on the worn rope at the edge of the swaying bridge, her black eyes shrouded with sadness. Death is bored with this. He wants to done this contract and go home for his dinner. He cleans his gun. I hear the catch go "click click." I see the sparks from his eyes as he loads the lead.

"Take the bag, man," she says. I look at Death, his brazen brass-face self all exposed now coming with his twisted gold-teeth smile down the other end of the swinging bridge. I look at the goddamn bag. I know it's all she has. The fool-fool thing is dragging her into the river and she is still struggling to hold on to it. And so I kiss my teeth and take the whatsitnotsit bag. "Open it," she says.

I open the cracked leather and I open the drawers. In each of the drawers there are delicate old green and blue glass bottles with poems neatly folded inside. And between the bottles there are round cardboard pillboxes with words like "intravenous" and "arterial" packed in them. In the silver boxes, are all the colours of the Rio Nuevo valley and the Blue Mountains and the scraps from my grandmother's sewing and the recipes for the natural remedies my great-great-grandfather sold at Apothecary Hall in Savanna la Mar.

My mother and I dance a duet on the swinging bridge and the old man from the mento band cross the river raises his battered violin and the guitar men come in and the tempo of the rhumba box is triumphant and the women from the Church of Zion come with their drummer to dance too — dressed in white, yellow pencils in their red headties and their wide skirts spin out like shelters for the homeless. And my mother smiles because she has given me what I need and I can cross the bridge alone at last. I hold her close and feel her tears on my neck. She who never cries. And the women are singing *Rock O/ Rock Holy/ Mount Zion children/ Rock Holy.*

Then Death taps his walking stick and the gun salute begins. *Bye bye bye bye bye* — fireworks in the daylight. He puts his cloak on her as she falls and lifts her high in his stiltman's arms and they go through the field of red ginger, through the red mud of the mountain between the ackee and the macafat palm up up up into the blue hilltops where the mist covers them.

And I am crossing the Rio Nuevo swinging bridge alone, heavy with my bag of poems, my medical words, my colours, my scraps and herbs and the songs of the revival women to sing me home.

Coda

I

Gynaecologies

After the funeral came the sorting out.
I wanted to keep the patients' cards. The gynaecologies
of several prime minister's wives (opposing parties),
medical histories of the lovers of retired politicians too,
the documentation of domestic violence among the middle classes,
the physical sufferings of household helpers.
(Bill: Mrs. E. Chang, employer),
the resistances and accommodations to obeah and myal.

We burned them.

It was the way you did things, true to the rules
of the scholarship you learned: the blush pink cards
from the sixties surgery. I had the historian's instinct.
Or the priest's. Save them. You'd kept them for twenty years,
after all, you must've done it for a reason.
But you believed in that old Greek oath and kept it;
confidentiality, the secrets of the talking cure,
laboratory evidence never crawled out of your mouth, Ma.

I sat reading them.
Holding them in my hands.
And then as you had cut the cord, I cut it too.

I took five hundred cards,
("The Health practices of Post Colonial Jamaica"),
 threw them into the gully and lit them.

A week later, the day I had to
catch the plane back to Toronto
I woke up wanting them. I went to look.
Maybe I could salvage even ten.
I'd give them to a library.
Some researcher could use them.

They were there, under the old guango tree,
neat, shell-like layers of ash, dark and mute as
the registrar's handwriting on your death certificate
"Sex: female. Occupation: none".

My
Mother's
Last Dance

II

Pentimento

Snow blankets the avenue
smothers the noise of the children's games
below the window where I am looking
across the avenue   across the turquoise sea
to the green and black cliffs   of the Rio Nuevo valley
into a light-filled bush alive with doctor birds,
pea doves and pitcharie, sprinkled with
rainbow colours these avenue children have never seen.
Deep magenta bouganvillaea, and the rich ochre of croton
flecked with amber burn through the ice.

And all my history softly rises,
rises in the flowering snow; my mother in her green coat,
blood on her white rubber boots after a delivery,
her stethoscope cold against my chest,
the inflatable assemblage of tubes and pipes
for clearing stubborn or obstructed ovarian tubes
my Grandmother, severe and serious
sprinkling shards of coconut,
chanting to the doomed chickens

"Kopleng kopleng kopleng
coop coop coop
Speck Leck, Senseh fowl, Reddy and ole hen"
Pimento dram to ease your cramp

ginger tea to belch off the gas
and help yuh fight life gwan. The two mothers
skeletal as the white bark of pimento,
are entwined with the rich blooms of thumbergia or alamander
looping in and out of the dark earth, their bones
seed laden, powdery and soft as dried arrowroot.

The Toronto avenue might seem charged
with the absence of these things
were it not for their uneasy presence in the pentimento
of my mind's canvas, as if in flicking cable channels
you could surf between past and present
destroy history's shadow, re-invent the here and now
grafted and sutured from atavistic fragments
whose hideousness or beauty is marked
by a momentary grey nothingness:
the act of violence giving rise to the imperfect act of love.

Now it is spring. The children
are searching out the seeds ripening near the sidewalk
and the armies of trees marching out
of the women's ashes in the earth.

*My
Mother's
Last Dance*

Acknowledgements

GRATEFUL ACKNOWLEDGEMENT is made to those who first published some of the poems in this book.

ANNA TAURUS and MAMEE (now retitled THE SURVEYOR) © 1983 from *Focus* 1983 ed. Mervyn Morris, Caribbean Authors Publishing Co. Ltd., Kingston, Jamaica. LALA THE DRESSMAKER © 1982 from *An Anthology of African and Caribbean Writing in English* ed. John Figueroa, Heinemann Educational Books Ltd in association with the Open University, London, Ibadan, Nairobi, Kingston and Port of Spain. A MESSAGE FROM NI and AUX LEON WOMEN © 1990 from *Creation Fire: A Cafra Anthology of Caribbean Women's Poetry* ed. Ramabai Espinet, Sister Vision: Black Women and Women of Colour Press, Toronto, Canada. HISTORY'S POSSE © 1993 from *Canadian Women's Studies Special Issue on Women Writing*, Fall 1993 Vol 14 #1 York University, Toronto, Canada. MY MOTHER'S LAST DANCE © 1994 *The Massachusetts Review* Vol XXXV, No 3 and 4, Autumn-Winter 1994, University of Massachusetts: Amherst.